Food Memories

Life in Context: Telling Your Story

Workbook One

Melissa Mannon, MSLS
Archivist and Cultural Heritage Consultant

Sue West
Certified Organizer Coach®

Copyright © 2012 by Melissa Mannon and Sue West.

This work is subject to copyright. All rights reserved. No part of this publication may be reproduced, storied in a retrieval system or transmitted in any form or by any means, electronic, mechanical, photocopying, recording, scanning, or otherwise.

Food Memories. A Workbook from the Life in Context: Telling Your Story Series / Melissa Mannon and Sue West.

ISBN: 978-0-9827276-4-5

www.LifeinContext.org
www.OrganizeNH.com
www.ArchivesInfo.com

Melissa Mannon
ArchivesInfo
Melissa@ArchivesInfo.com
(603) 661-7611

Archivist and Cultural Heritage Consultant Melissa Mannon Melissa has twenty years of experience focused on archives management, community building, and cultural literacy. Her work encourages cultural heritage organizations to work collaboratively with local governments, businesses, and individuals who keep records in order to identify archives and plan for their care.

Sue West
Space4U Organizing
Sue@OrganizeNH.com
(603) 765-9267

Sue West of Space4U, Organizing Services, llc is a Certified Professional Organizer® & Certified Organizer Coach®. Through coaching, onsite organizing, and classes, Sue works with people to simplify, declutter and organize their lives, so that they have time for what's important to them. Her specialty is dealing with life's changes - supporting people moving through mid-life and later-life transitions, such as downsizing, loss of a partner/spouse, health issues, adult AD/HD diagnosis, the empty nest stage, and pre-retirement into retirement.

A Life in Context: Telling Your Story -- Food Memories Workbook

Contents

Part 1 - The Groundwork: About Food Memories 6
    Workbook Series Genesis 7
    Food and Culture 9
        Sample 1: Melissa's Bagel Food Memory 11
        Sample 2: Sue's Rice Krispy Treats Food Memory 12

Part 2 – Discovering Your Favorites 14
    Worksheet: Food Memories 15
    Food Biography 16
        Article: Write your own food biography: my life in 10 dishes. 17
        Exercise: Write Your Food Biography 21
    Sifting Through Memories 22
    Worksheet: Recording a Memory – Choosing One Food 24
    Food Related Items 25
        Sample 3: Creamsicles 26
    Worksheet: Related Information – Food Event 27
    Worksheet: Related Information – Food Items 28
        Sample 4: Thanksgiving at the Wests 29

Part 3– Putting It All Together - Your Memories in Context 30
    Worksheet: Children's Food Memories 31
    All About Me is All About Us 32
        Sample 5: Sue's Family Recipe Boxes, in Context 34
    Worksheet: Cultural Context 36

What's Next? Share Your Memories. 45
Would You Like to Share What You Have Explored Here? 47

Look backward to move forward.

Decide what to keep in your story and what to let go.

Think about your life in a whole new way.

Spend time with two local experts, an archivist & a professional organizer.

- Connect your present with your past. Honor it, without getting stuck
- Of all the memories you have, decide which are key to pass on
- Understand which belongings are important to your family history
- Understand how your memories fit into your broader community and culture
- Discover ways to record/document your own story, *a life in context*

You do not need to be a "writer" to record your memories. This is about sharing our stories and building community.

Part 1 - The Groundwork: About Food Memories

Sue West, Organizing Coach, and Melissa Mannon, Archivist, have combined their expertise to develop the *Life in Context Project.* The Project explores ways you can organize and evaluate objects by using them to relate the heirloom stories that highlight your values and culture.

The ultimate goal of the *Life in Context Project* is to help you understand, document, and pass on what is important to you. *Life in Context* began as a workshop, but it has truly become a "project." Our collaborative endeavor to explore personal and community memories through objects invites participation through any or all of a number of outlets. These outlets currently include tailored workshops, an online Facebook community, and Life in Context workbooks such as *Food Memories* that invite written submissions.

We continually strive to develop more ways to organize memories, and to share personal and community history. We welcome your participation and feedback. See www.LifeInContext.org to learn more about the project and take part!

Why we do what we do:

Melissa – I have always loved history. I have always connected it to me, but have also learned in this business that others don't always make that connection. I have gone from working with cultural institutions to helping individuals recognize that we all need to see ourselves as the center of history. Learn history backwards by thinking about your own life. Then, consider the historic events that helped create the context that made the life you live possible.

Food for me has always been a launching point for family stories. Meal times, especially those related to special occasions, were a time for relating memories and imparting family traditions.

Sue – A French major in college, I read Marcel Proust's *Remembrance of Things Past*, in which the Madeleine cookies and their aroma inspired memories he'd long forgotten. This idea of food provoking memories made a strong impression on me.

My general interest in history began with family genealogy and listening to the stories of my grandmother. Widowed quite young, she spent a great deal of time with me, as I grew up. I now support people with simplifying their lives. I've heard so many stories about people's belongings and have been curious: how do we preserve these stories and not lose the culture we are creating for our children, grandchildren and future historians.

Workbook Series Genesis

Figure 1 Photo of unidentified family picnicking.

This is our **first in a series of workbooks and workshops** to help you document what is meaningful to you.

We began thinking about "Food Memories" as a possible initial focus for *The Life in Context Project* topic in early 2011. Thinking about a winter release for this workbook perhaps had us thinking about the hearty warm New England foods that come out of our kitchens that time of year. Melissa was also inspired at that time by a museum colleague's project called [1] "The Pickle Project" that focused on local foods in the Ukraine. Plus, we found a food biography exercise online that got our mind wheels turning. (See page 18.) It all fit! Food memories seemed like a natural launching point.

Why do we eat the things we eat and how do our meals reflect our life in context?

Food Memories examines the role of food in your life. Food memories are universal. We all have them, yet they all differ. These memories are based on what we like, where we grew up, our ethnicity, and other factors that help define who we are. So, while food memories are not unusual, each of us has a unique perspective that is worth considering, telling, and placing into context. This resource will help you consider the meals, the events, the heirloom serving pieces, and the places that define your precious food memories.

We began by exploring our own food memories – to compare and contrast our stories. This allowed us to better understand how food memories fit into the context or our lives. We then created and launched a contest about food memories for which we asked people to send in their stories. We wanted to learn more about the food memories in context and to for them serve as project samples. We were overjoyed at the response and so are sharing some of these memories in this book to inspire you. Our favorite memories are published here, alongside our tips for telling your story, organizing your food life, and preserving your heritage, as it relates to food.

---

[1] For more on the Pickle Project see:
http://archivesinfo.blogspot.com/2011/01/lost-stories-guest-post-by-linda-norris.html (December 16, 2011)

Figure 2 The Life in Context Facebook page

This contest, people told us, was the first time many had recorded their stories about favorite foods. And sometimes, that's what it takes – a manufactured deadline – to get us to tell our stories. Our call for stories through the "Life in Context" Facebook page challenged the following:

Write two to four paragraphs about a food related object that is important to you. Record your memory associated with it. (We told people to feel free to write in paragraph form, answering each question. Or, weave the questions into a personal story. We suggested that they may prefer to put ideas in a bulleted list if they didn't fancy writing. We wanted to make it as easy as possible for people to contribute!)

Consider if there are people involved with this memory. Why are these people important to this particular memory?

Do you have related documentation? Can this be put into a cultural context? When did this happen? To what community does this relate?

We also offered a worksheet for helping people gather their thoughts. The worksheet was intended to serve as a launching point for creating a sort of biography through food. The questions have been split up and explained in this publication. Throughout this book we will offer more tips and details for recording your food memories. Contributed stories begin on page 37.

Food and Culture

Culture is the customs, beliefs, social mores, and material traits of a community. Culture is what your community holds dear or that which gives your group its identity.

Figure 3 "Tea time"
©Melissa Mannon, 2008

Food is a vital part of culture. Our food heritage -- the dishes themselves, the dining company we keep, the places we associate with a good meal, our heirloom serving items, and more -- reflect our cultural identity, giving us a sense of who we are and what is important to us.

Food is part of the culture that cultural heritage professionals refer to as "intangible" because many of our food traditions are not recorded and are passed from generation to generation by word of mouth or by live demonstration. For example, I know how to cook a meatball properly (the Italian way) because my Italian mother-in-law stood in the kitchen with me and showed me how her mother showed her. (*Melissa*)

Think about the foods you eat that have special meaning to you because they were passed down by your family or were integral parts of your community life. Consider what foods represent your heritage and how that heritage has been passed on to you. Did you learn to cook standing at your mother's side? Do you have a dog-eared, food splattered recipe book that once belonged to your grandmother? Do you have the sedar plate or the Christmas cookie platter that served your family well for generations? Is there a dish that reminds you of a favorite community eatery? This book offers you the opportunity to explore behind your everyday food experiences to discover the more meaningful side of sustenance. Why do we eat the things we eat and how do our meals reflect our life in context?

We can think of the context of our lives in two parts: a little context and a big context. Our little context considers each of us at our very core. Who are you? What do you like? What specific memories do you have? The foods and food related things we like give some insight about us. You are a person who prefers salt or sweet. You may like to cook. You may prefer to go out to a restaurant. Those closest to each of us know our preferences and may acknowledge our food desires by serving us certain meals or helping us create food habits that suit our schedule.

The second part is a larger context. Who are you and who is in your community? What do you like to eat and how does it reflect your ethnicity, geography, or other community group? Do you like certain foods because they are part of your community? What specific memories do you have about certain foods and do other members of your community have related memories? How do your community's memories differ from people in differing communities?

The rest of this book explores ways to examine the meaning that food plays in your life and to determine what foods are most significant to you. When you begin thinking about the value of your activities, your traditions, and objects, you begin to piece together a puzzle that provides a better understanding of your role and your place in the world. Understanding your food heritage is a vital piece of this puzzle because food says so much about your values and your culture. Indeed, you are what you eat!

There is much value in considering the foods that are meaningful to you. It can help you recognize that your identity is rooted in a heritage that can evoke personal pride. It can make it easier to pass on your memories (and your recipes) to your loved ones. It even can help you to teach and pass on your morals, beliefs, and ideas. Since what we eat often grows out of who we are, the stories associated with specific foods can reflect our core values.

Many people we meet in our respective consulting businesses tell us that they didn't realize that their things or their memories may have value to others. In fact, your memories are not only valuable to you and your family—they have historical importance to your communities as well. The food memories we examine in this book are just one aspect of your life story that other people want to hear to help them better understand their own lives in context.

By sharing stories, we gain understanding of our foods in a community context. A community is a formal or informal group with a common history or culture. Every individual participates in communities, either intentionally or unintentionally, through ethnicity, living space, workplaces, beliefs, and behaviors. Your food memories are part of a larger community memory. Together, our community food memories help us understand the groups to which we belong, how these groups intersect with others, and the similarities and differences among people. Examining our food culture and comparing it to those of others helps us define ourselves and the world around us. Melissa works with museums, libraries, and archives – so-called "cultural memory institutions" that work to document and preserve just the kind of memories this workbook examines.

Sample 1: Melissa's Bagel Food Memory

Figure 4 "Not My Breakfast"
©Melissa Mannon, 2006

A heavenly smell would fill the air when my mother brought back a bag from the bagel store in our neighborhood. Such places dotted the retail areas where I grew up on Long Island in New York State. Behind the counters were multiple flavors of cream cheese and lox. Most commonly in my parents' home, we ate the breadstuffs with butter and plain cream cheese. On weekends, we would slap cold cuts between a sliced bagel or turn it into a pizza with sauce and cheese. We used cherry preserves (the kind with the fat red fruit spread throughout the sweet sticky goo) around Passover time when we also ate the treat on our matzo. Once in awhile, mom would excitedly shuffle her three kids off to school and run to the gourmet bagel shop for special flavors to share with her girlfriends over morning tea. I spent the day hoping that some flavors -- maybe chocolate, chives or pineapple -- would be left for us to sample when we got home.

I remember the bagels, but I can barely remember how they tasted and I cannot eat them anymore. My daughter will readily tell you the story. I have a photo essay that I made to hang in my kitchen when I was first diagnosed. I made a collage of four separate pictures of four different off-limits breakfasts. My daughter finds this quite funny, in a way that only a small seven year old can find such things funny. "Remember that photo that was in the kitchen that you called 'Not My Breakfast' since you can't eat those things because you have Celiac Disease, Mom?" She smiles at me as if she is proud that she understands this inside joke that tries to convey my loss of bagels to the world. This beautiful girl was impossible for me to conceive ten years ago because of a disease that went undiagnosed for twenty years (even though it is considered the number one case of unexplained infertility.) My daughter does not understand the full irony.

When a person is diagnosed with Celiac - a disorder that makes the body unable to process the gluten protein found in wheat, barley and rye – that person needs to eliminate the offending foods entirely from the diet. At first, it is a difficult thing to do. Some, like me, even get nauseous at the smell of bread for a short time. I remember walking into a bagel shop during my "recovery" period to get some lunch for my husband. I had to turn around and walk out because of my physical discomfort. It was as if my favorite food had turned on me, until I put a new spin on it and realized it was just warning me away like an old friend looking out for my best interest.

To me, a bagel is one sign in my life that represents a lot. It embodies my Jewish heritage and my New York upbringing. It also stands for what I now cannot eat. It represents the struggle I went through to become a mother and to live a healthy, normal life. My daughter does not hope for me to save her some of my special food when I shuffle her off to school. Instead she anticipates that I will think of her and stop in the local bakery to get her a fancy sugar cookie...New Hampshire bagels are just not the same as New York ones anyway.

> "Tell me what you eat and I will tell you what you are."
>
> Jean Anthelme Brillat-Savarin
> (famous 18th century foodie)

Sample 2: Sue's Rice Krispy Treats Food Memory

Figure 5 Great Aunt Ludy and Great Aunt Esther

Rice Krispy Treats are back in vogue! At a favorite restaurant & café recently, the dessert tray included a childhood favorite, Rice Krispy Treats – only with a different twist. The treat had a peanut butter layer, with chocolate frosting. Like Proust and his Madeleines, I was transported to my childhood.

Great Aunts Ludy and Esther, "the girls" as my mother and her mother called the unmarried sisters, always made and brought Rice Krispy treats to our Christmas together, along with homemade fudge. They had started their tradition in the days when my grandmother hosted Christmas, which would have begun in the 1950's.

My great aunts lived in the Brookline, Massachusetts home in which all six Richardson children had been born, a home their father had built. I remember the high ceilings, the secret passage way from the second floor to the kitchen, the long bannister we slid down, and the very warm room on the third floor with pictures on the wall of Nixon, Agnew (politicians) and Jess Cain, a Boston radio personality.

They were the biggest of Red Sox fans, taking the subway into games at Fenway Park, Boston until Ludy and Esther were well into their 80's. They had season tickets as far back as my mother can remember. Season tickets were unusual for two women in those days! They inspired me because they did what they wanted to do, because of their curiosity, intelligence and their senses of humor.

For work, Ludy was high up in ranks of the Girl Scouts in New England, Girl Scouts being a long tradition in my family is now carried on with my young niece. Esther worked for the Universalist Association. In the year before I was born (1959), my mother worked across the street from Aunt Esther in Boston. Mom worked for the Unitarian association, for Dana McLean Greeley, who became the first president of the merger of Unitarian and Universalist churches. Again, as with the Girl Scouts there is a long history of Unitarianism in my family, including several talented ministers.

My great aunts lived into their 90's. Esther had a lively sense of humor and was the rebel of the two of them. Ludy was more structured and appeared to like it that way. So they made a wonderful pair. In their later years, Ludy would become Esther's caregiver at their childhood home. And then it was a sad Christmas day, that year following Esther's death; Ludy did not join us but sent just her own gift of the fudge.Kellogg's had created Rice Krispy cereal in 1928. Then in 1939, when Mildred Day, a Kellogg's employee and her friend Malitta needed an idea to help their Campfire Girls raise money, they put their heads together and a new delicious food was invented. It was Rice Crispy Treats!

In 2001, students working on Iowa State's annual spring celebration a record-breaking - and tasty - event the world's biggest Rice Krispy Treat. ISU is the alma mater of Mildred Day.

Resources:

- From Wikipedia: history, marketing, cultural impacts: http://en.wikipedia.org/wiki/Rice_Krispies (link verified December 16, 2011)
- From Wikipedia, about the treats: http://en.wikipedia.org/wiki/Rice_Krispies_treat (link verified December 16, 2011)
- The original recipe: http://www.ricekrispies.com/recipes/the-original-treats.aspx#/recipes/the-original-treats (link verified December 16, 2011)

Part 2 – Discovering Your Favorites

This section will help you sort through your own memories. The exercises and questions will help you to identify which of these memories are most important to you, so that you may then focus on telling your story. People are often overwhelmed when asked to choose a "favorite." Instead, we aim to help you recognize the foods that have some personal or cultural meaning to you. The food might be related to your childhood or to a special occasion or a favorite restaurant. Your ancestors might have passed it down through many generations. It might be a new recipe tradition you have adopted for your own family or a new tradition begun with a local restaurant's food. It could even be a food related memory and not a specific meal. Perhaps you have a special serving dish or a special place to eat or a food you cook that fills you with warm thoughts. If you're like us, you have many favorite foods. Knowing this, let us not try to choose THE favorite. Let's aim to identify a group of favorites. We eventually want to record just one memory in detail, but we do not need to do that just yet. Here we will guide you to:

- Choose your first food memory to record;
- Reflect on why this food is important to you;
- Sift through your memories by talking to others and reviewing information you have.

You have read our examples of food memories. No doubt you now have some of your own ideas about food objects or recipes that came to you while reading our stories. Let's quickly capture those ideas. Without putting too much thought into it, jot down some foods that you immediately think of as significant to you:

_____

_____

_____

To move forward with one of these ideas, to explore others, and to figure out with which food memory you would like to use to get started, we offer you three different approaches:

1. Use the worksheet with questions on the next page.

2. Write a "food biography." Read the article, page 17 and write your food biography on page 21. See sample food bios from Melissa and Sue at http://www.lifeincontext.org/Foodbios.php

3. Review your recipes and cookbooks collection. Use our worksheet, page 22.

Worksheet: Food Memories

Think about the foods with which you cook or the dishes that you enjoy today. Make a list of the favorite meals that come immediately to mind. Don't think too hard about it. Just record what comes up.

_____

_____

Think about and list some of the foods you ate as child. Do you still make or eat any of these as an adult?

_____

_____

Have any of these foods been passed down through your family?

_____

_____

Are there specific food related items that have significance to you? Is there a special serving dish or utensil? What is it and how is it important to you?

_____

_____

What places (restaurants, family member's kitchens, vegetable gardens, etc.) hold warm food related memories for you?

_____

_____

_____

Food Biography

Intangible heritage includes the parts of one's culture that are not consciously recorded. Examples are music, language, dance, and food. This type of heritage is often passed down by communities from one generation to the next. A culture can easily lose its intangible heritage. The loss usually happens when someone breaks the chain by not revealing these cultural elements to someone else. For example, Melissa's mother-in-law taught her at the kitchen stove how to properly make an Italian meatball. Alternately, her grandmother made brisket and brought it to the table already prepared with soft carrots and potatoes. Melissa remembers the meal fondly, but never learned Grandma's recipe, which is now lost to time.

While developing the *Life in Context Project*, we were inspired by the idea of a food diary. The exercise, described in the article on the following pages, prompts you to think about the meals that have some significance to you and is another way to start exploring your life in the context of food. These foods may have been made by grandma or taught to you by your mother-in-law. Menu items at your favorite restaurant or treats from your favorite bakery during your days as a foreign exchange student in France give you a beginning point for exploration.

This exercise gives you a chance to think about the tastes and smells that have influenced you and to consider their cultural context. Now is your chance to write down the bones of what has not previously been recorded. (And perhaps once you have thought about your favorite dishes, you may take this to the next level and make sure you have the recipe written down somewhere!)

This method could be particularly useful to people who do not like to write. Make a bulleted list or consider creating a collage of words or pictures. We have left a blank page at the end of the article so that you can create your own food diary page right in this book in the form that suits you best.

Article: Write your own food biography: my life in 10 dishes[2].

Jill Dupleix, Table Talk blog
July 29, 2010

There are lots of ways of tracing your own personal history. You can go back through family photo archives and trace the hair styles. You can do it with music, by listing the songs that symbolize special times in your life. Or you can do it with food. Food has an incredible power to evoke the past; to remind us of special occasions, disasters and triumphs, and those long gone. I think of my father every time I grill a lamb chop on the barbie[3], and of my grandmother every time I smell porridge cooking.

To write your own food biography, come up with ten dishes from your past to your present, from your very first food memory to your current obsession. Write them down. They don't have to be the best ten best dishes you've ever had in your life, just represent you at certain ages and stages. That's your entire life there, plate after plate.

Your list will be different to mine, and different to your nearest and dearest. A stranger could look at them and know so much about you and your life; where you came from, who you became, and everything in between. The places you have lived will be in there, the people you have loved and who have loved you. Every dish tells a story, good or bad.

Here are mine.

First important dish: Porridge.

My grandmother, Dolly May Campbell, was born in Queensland of Scottish descent. She fell in love with the 'jackaroo' on her family property, and they travelled around Australia, he managing properties, she running the household, until settling in the Western District of Victoria. She was a brilliant porridge maker and I used to love staying with her overnight so we could have porridge for breakfast. She had a small red enamel pan (her entire kitchen was fitted out in bright red) and a number of wooden spoons that were worn down almost diagonally in half from all the stirring. I'll never forget how heavenly that porridge smelt.

---

[2] Permission granted: Jill Dupleix, Table Talk blog, theage.com.au and smh.com.au (Fairfax Media), July 2010 (links verified December 16, 2011.)

[3] *"Barbie" is a short-hand word, in Australia, for barbecue or grill.

Greek meatballs.

Second dish: Definitely egg and bacon pie.

It came out of the oven when we were on holidays, when we went off on picnics, when we went water-skiing at the local lake, and became synonymous with good times when the entire family was together.

Third dish: Lamb chops, mashed potatoes and peas.

Growing up on a sheep farm meant we had lamb and mutton pretty much non-stop, in a roll call that went from roast lamb on Sundays to cold lamb salads on Monday, lamb fritters with tomato sauce on Tuesdays, lamb curry with sultanas on Wednesdays. I always loved the grilled lamb chops (with 'tails'), mashed potatoes and peas the best. Mum always let us kids choose the menu for our birthday dinners, and I remember her apologizing to my grandmother for serving her such a modest meal at my tenth birthday, because I had requested my favourite.

Fourth dish: Sausages and honey.

Off to boarding school, which was a bit of a shock to the system, not least because after three years at a co-ed high school, it was an all-girl establishment. And because of the food. Trays of greasy fried eggs for Sunday breakfast, savoury mince that was as pale as the tablecloth, gristly stews, thin soups – no wonder I used to more than my body weight of white bread and jam sandwiches. It sounds weird, but the otherwise delicious thin, crisp-skinned beef breakfast sausages were so shiny with grease, that we used to douse them in honey (okay, it might have been just me) to make them edible. I have, on occasion, reproduced this pairing as an adult, but not while in a public place.

Fifth dish: Tiropites, little triangular filo pastries filled with feta and spinach.

I was so proud of myself. I had survived boarding school, had a great job as an advertising copywriter, and was living in Melbourne in the tiniest ever inner-city cottage. I had a mad passion for all things Greek, and my first ever overseas trip planned - to Greece - with my girlfriend. We'd eat our way up and down Swan Street, planning all the things we were going to do on holidays. I'd invite friends over and make huge batches of tiropites. I suspect it was the only thing I could make, so I just kept making it.

Sixth dish: My Pub Roast.

It went like this: put leg of lamb and heaps of potatoes in the oven to cook, and go to the pub. Have such a good time that by the time you come back hours later the lamb is completely crisped and the potatoes are incredibly crunchy and golden and completely hollow. Eat.

Seventh dish: Oeufs poule aux caviar (Eggs in eggs).

I fell in love, not with a handsome Greek man in Greece, but with a mad Australian man called Terry (at the pub, of course) just weeks before I was to leave. I never went. We started living together, cooking and eating and drinking. We bought cookbooks and equipment and had a go at just about everything: breads, pickles, incredibly complicated nouvelle cuisine, and lots of charcuterie, fuelled by our first trip to France. My dinner party special was Michel Guerard's caviar with creamed eggs, of creamy scrambled eggs and chives piled into hollowed-out egg shells, topped with caviar and served with toast soldiers. It all felt very chic.

Seventh dish: Gougeres.

Still on the French kick, although by now I was into hearty, rustic regional food rather than cheffy stuff. I'd been to Burgundy and eaten these enormous, puffy, cheesy choux pastries fresh from a bakery on a hilly street of Vezelay and fallen in love with them. But I was still scared of words like 'choux' and 'pastry'. Determined to conquer my fear, I had a go at heating water, butter and salt, dumping in the flour and beating like mad until the dough left the sides of the pan. Then I threw it in my trusty food processor, added eggs and whizzed, added cheese and dropped spoonfuls onto a tray and baked them – and they worked. I felt invincible. I Had Made Gougeres. Then I invited some chefs around for dinner, added one egg too many to the mixture, and lost the lot. Sigh.

Only my mother will still be reading this by now, but I don't particularly care – I'm having such a beautiful time reliving these amazing dishes, each one a stepping stone to who I am and how I cook today.

Eighth dish: Sticky toffee pudding.

What a great dish this is. When you analyse it, it's just a date cake covered in caramel sauce, but why analyse it when you can eat it. At this stage I was doing an ABC radio recipe segment on what was then called 3LO – the night I ran through the sticky toffee pudding recipe the switchboard jammed as the ABC was hit with requests – they handed out over 500 recipes that night alone. There were some quite important political events happening around that time, but we the people had decided a good pud was far more important.

Ninth dish: Flourless chocolate cake.

The best, the one and only, the finest chocolate cake in the world. It is now linked so irrevocably with the great celebratory occasions and happy times of my life that every time I even think about it, I smile.

Tenth dish: Greek meatballs.

Yep, I finally got to Greece, with the man I met in the pub. We went all over Mykonos trying to find our Melbourne/Greek version of a great Greek meal– grilled pita bread and tarama salata, Greek salad and grilled fish. Then we stopped for the most amazing meatballs ever at a beautiful restaurant called Mamacas, which makes a point of doing home-made, motherly cooking. They were so stunning, so large and light and smothered in sweetly spiced tomato sauce, that we've been making them like that at home ever since.

So my food-biography has gone full circle. Already. I asked Terry for his, and he rattled off:

1/ Tinned smoked oysters on Savoy crackers
2/ Neapolitan ice-cream
3/ Hungarian chicken giblet soup with carrots and egg noodles
4/ Coronation chicken (chicken in creamy curry sauce)
5/ Ma po beancurd
6/ Cassoulet with duck confit
7/ Tarte fine aux pommes
8/ Andouillette, pomme frites and mustard
9/ Grilled pig's trotters stuffed with chicken farce, morels
10/ Curry laksa

Well, that was fun. Now we want to hear about your stepping stones – what dishes are special to you and why? All good food comes with a story, and the stories need sharing as much as the food.

Read more: http://www.theage.com.au/entertainment/blogs/table-talk/write-your-own-food-biography-my-life-in-10-dishes-20100729-10xrd.html#ixzz1eWkUXpXe (link verified December 16, 2011)

Exercise: Write Your Food Biography

1. Your earliest food memory:

   _____

2. _____

3. _____

4. _____

5. _____

6. _____

7. _____

8. _____

9. _____

10. Your most recent food memory:

    _____

Sifting Through Memories

Sometimes, it will be easier to choose a food memory with which to start by reviewing what you already have! The act of organizing our things or examining our thoughts can spur us on to write. Getting your thoughts in order can also help you choose just one memory on which to focus.

First things first[4]: Bring to one place all of your recipes and cookbooks from:

- Kitchen and dining room bookshelves or hutch;
- Your computer: do you save recipes people send you? Bookmark favorite sites?
- Recipe boxes, especially popular for recipes handed down in families;
- Folders of recipes torn out from magazines or newspapers;
- Menus from favorite restaurants.

It may be that THE recipe is right there in front of you because for you, just seeing the cookbook cover, recipe, or menu is enough to spark your memory.[5]

Or you might want to talk to loved ones to help bring out memories. Sue talked with her mother about holiday traditions to figure out what to write about for her food memory. The discussion eventually led Sue to choose to write about Rice Krispy Treats. She did a verbal "sift through" of her family memories over the phone.

Or, your "sift through" could become part of a larger project. The year Sue's mom and dad were downsizing, her mom did her own sifting through as a result of the larger goal of an eventual move. She passed to Sue the role of hosting Thanksgiving, along with the family objects. These included the Thanksgiving centerpiece, a silver appetizer platter from two generations ago, the recipes, and mom's childhood book about the Pilgrims -- a book they read to each child as he/she grows up in the family. Or, do as one of Sue's clients did. She used our food memories contest to "sift through" and declutter all of her recipes and cookbooks. First, at her dining room table, her client made piles: often-used recipes; favorite family recipes; recipes out of use; and cookbooks that were gifts, but never really left the shelf. After she finished her "sifting through," it was easy to see that her food memory was most likely going to be in the "favorite family recipes" group. So she narrowed down her collection first, then looked at all her options for choosing which food memory to record.

---

[4] For more ideas about simplifying your life, particularly after a big life change, preview Sue's book, Organize for a Fresh Start: Embrace Your Next Chapter in Life at www.OrganizeForAFreshStart.com

[5] Eating out or bringing food in can play a significant role in our memories of food. See the New York Public Library's "What's on the Menu" project for one way we explore what people "were eating back in the day." http://menus.nypl.org/

Which written recipes reflect warm memories of family?

_____

_____

_____

Who else do you know who might have memories of these foods and events?

_____

_____

_____

What traditions are represented in your things? Have you thought about passing these down to another family member (as Sue's mom did as Thanksgiving host?)

_____

_____

_____

Consider your recipes. Determine which you use monthly, which are occasional, which you don't use, which are true family gems that you want to hand down. Make a list here of your heirloom recipes that you would like to hand down or favorite eateries to purchase beloved foods.

_____

_____

Consider food that you bring in that becomes part of a tradition. List them here. (For example, in Melissa's childhood home, friends visiting from NYC would always bring Italian cookies.)

_____

_____

Worksheet: Recording a Memory – Choosing One Food

Now, identify one food with which you would like to start. Choose the one that inspires you at this moment. You do not need to consider if it is THE most important or THE favorite. Just choose something that is sitting in your brain with thoughts waiting to tumble out.

Write that food here. _____

As you consider recording your memories, use all of your senses in your effort. This makes your story come alive to others reading it.

Jot down your initial thoughts here using key words or sentences and paragraphs. Write how this food is important to you. Record a memory that relates to this food What makes this memorable for you?

_____

_____

_____

Who else is involved with this memory? How are these people important to this particular memory? How are they important to who you are or to your life today?

_____

_____

_____

Where and when did this memory happen – at your home, a restaurant, a gathering? Place the food or food-related items into a context: place, time of year, stage of your life.

_____

_____

_____

Food Related Items

We have begun exploring the recorded information we already have about food by reviewing our recipe files and cookbooks. But foods show up in other places we might not immediately consider such as in:

- Photos
- Videos
- Diary entries
- Menus
- Flyers
- Arts and crafts

Figure 6 Photo of an unidentified community event

A wedding is an example of a life experience that generates a lot of food related memories. Consider how one might record wedding memories through a food lens: include the tasting menu, caterer information, description of cakes tasted, the wine list or what was served at the bar, photos of food, video of cake cutting, close up of strawberry stain on bride's dress. (Melissa has a memory of tasting chocolate covered strawberries at her wedding that took place over seventeen years ago. She found a strawberry stain on the dress when she hung it in the closet after the event. She believes the stain is still there and it's about time she had that dress cleaned and preserved as best she can at this point!)

Think beyond the food itself. Evaluate what items you have that help tell the story and then consider how they can be used to highlight what is important to you. Original documents and objects – even ones with flaws -- can be used to tell your story in a unique way. (Just like the seemingly meaningless and annoying strawberry stain on a dress.)

Create a family archive of material related to a particular event. Put materials related to one event in a special "preservation safe" box, which gives you easy access to all the items that support your memories.

Consider using your materials in unique ways beyond a typical "archive." [6] Melissa often makes photo collages to combine ideas she values. We have friends who make quilts and do other creative crafty projects to tell family stories.

The example and story below are from a professional photographer and writer. She is the creator of the popular blog "My Artful Life," exploring and sharing the world around her through creativity that often involves objects. At this writing, she is experimenting with online collage building to tell stories.

Sample 3: Creamsicles

My siblings and I managed to survive childhood without a family car. Living on an island that measures four miles by nine meant that during the summers, we lived on our bicycles.

Figure 7 Lisa Allen's ingredients for a Creamsicle Protein Smoothie

My favorite ice cream treat, the creamsicle, was most often purchased at the Children's Beach snack bar, a daily pit stop for my brother and me. What fun it was to slurp the melting orange-flavored ice and vanilla ice cream before it slid off the stick.

The VitaMix is a high-powered blender that can juice an entire orange, skin included. My Creamsicle Protein Smoothie is the perfect marriage of adult nutrition and childhood indulgence.

- Lisa Allen http://www.lisaallenlambert.com (link verified December 16, 2011)

---

[6] To keep your family information safe, be sure (when possible) to make copies of original items for scrapbooking, shadow boxes, and the like. Original items can be greatly damaged and their information can be lost forever if you use them instead of copies. Store original materials away safely using "preservation safe" supplies from an online reputable supplier such as Gaylord Brothers, Metal Edge or University Products. Their products are designed specifically to keep your items safe for a long time.

Worksheet: Related Information – Food Event

Think about all of the places you experience food. Consider where special events such as weddings take place; family members' homes where holiday meals take place; favorite picnicking spots, etc. Consider some occasions that generated strong food memories and list them here:

_____

_____

_____

Put together a collection of materials related to a particular food event memory. Make a list of all pertinent materials. See our examples at the beginning of this section.

_____

_____

_____

After gathering your collection, consider how you can highlight the role that food plays in a memory by crafting or pursuing another creative project using your materials. What kinds of creative projects would you enjoy pursuing?

_____

_____

_____

What do you need to get started in this creative project? What or who can assist you?
_____

_____

_____

Worksheet: Related Information – Food Items

Make a list of heirloom food items that have been passed down to you by a family member or friend:

_____

_____

_____

Pick one item from this list and record its "provenance" – the people who owned the items before you and how it got to you:

_____

_____

_____

Write a memory that you have that is associated with this item. Do you remember a family member using it? Do you remember how it was given or presented to you? Do you remember any stories that a relative told you about how the item was used?

_____

_____

_____

Are you continuing a family tradition with this item? How do you use it? Does it differ from the way others used it before you?

_____

_____

_____

Sample 4: Thanksgiving at the Wests

Figure 8 Photo of Sue's family dinner table

(Sue) - At the age of 51, and shortly after one of my parents got through a significant health issue, I decided it was time to offer to host our family's Thanksgiving celebration. My parents thought it was a nice idea. Their trust in me to take over a valued family tradition was really the first part of my gift from them on that special occasion. Other parts of the gift showed up, with my parents, when they arrived on Thanksgiving day.

When I work with people and give my downsizing classes, I mention holidays as an example of a <u>manufactured deadline</u>. It's not quite the same as a self-imposed deadline, because a deadline to someone else is often easier to stick to. My parents easily could have let the date go by. At some future time, they would have told us to go through our stuff. But they used the date, Thanksgiving, as a motivator.

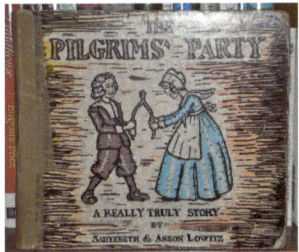 

My parents are gradually downsizing their 'stuff.' As with many of us in mid/later life, my parents also have my grandparents' belongings in their own home. It appears to me that mom is in charge of the "downsizing project." She is the one who makes the consignment, jeweler and other appointments and decides what goes where and to whom. I'm guessing that Dad advises a bit along the way when asked, and offers another perspective. He also works the deadlines with the three of us "chillens," as he lovingly calls us.

They brought some of the family "heirlooms" that enriched our holiday experience and my food memories. One gift was <u>The Pilgrims' Party</u> book in the picture, which at least three generations have read to the children on Thanksgiving Day. Another was my favorite silver platter which holds the celery, black olives, and green olives (which, as tradition has it, dad and I gobble up entirely before the meal begins!). And the other item was the Thanksgiving centerpiece, also pictured (yes, the "stuffed" turkey!)

Part 3– Putting It All Together - Your Memories in Context
Involving Your Children and Grandchildren: Our Food Tree of Thanks

Melissa - While walking on Thanksgiving morning, I was pondering a holiday tradition I keep every year with my daughter. We make a tree of thanks to remind us of all the things for which we are grateful. Our tree of thanks is drawn on a poster sized piece of paper and to that we glue leaves with our thoughts of thanks throughout the month of November.

This year, I decided to create a food tree of thanks, too. I decided to ask my elementary-aged child for the food items she could list that elicited memories for her. I told her that one example could be cake because it probably reminds her of birthday parties. She promptly listed a few others including: ice cream because it reminds her of her favorite babysitter who takes her to the local sweets stand; apples because they remind her of our cat who died earlier this year -- apples were his favorite food and we planted apple trees near his grave site; berries and nuts because they remind her of the birds and chipmunks we see out our windows every day; eating "free" ice cream sundaes on Wednesdays at one of her favorite restaurants.

Figure 9 The Tree of Thanks in early November. By the end of the season, the leaves fill the door.

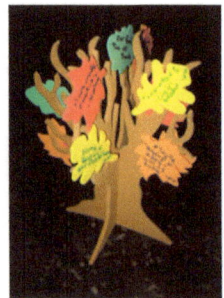

Figure 10 Our new food tree of thanks

The food tree of thanks is a fun way to include children in an exploration about food and memory. It can encourage an appreciation for history and may even assist with healthy eating by making kids think about why they eat what they eat.

On the next page are a few questions to incorporate into your conversation. These will help you create your own food tree of thanks and get your kids thinking about their own food related memories. Be aware that kids may need a little extra prompting. For example, the last question asks about people who make special foods for them. It's okay to say something such as, "Do I make special foods for you? What about Daddy? What about Grandma?" These prompts can help get their ideas flowing. (Prompting during oral history interviews with adults can sometimes be helpful too!)

Worksheet: Children's Food Memories

Which foods are special to you and remind you of special events like your birthday?

_____

_____

_____

How are these foods special to you? What makes them so special? Would you want to eat any of these foods all the time?

_____

_____

_____

Let's work together to make a list of the activities in which you like to participate and places you like to go (examples: dance, football games, hiking, play dates, etc.) Which foods remind you of these activities? How so?

_____

_____

_____

Do any of the people you love make you special foods that no one else makes for you? How or why do these foods remind you of them?

_____

_____

_____

All About Me is All About Us

Figure 11 Unidentified family at the "family table"

Put your memories into a context beyond you, either into a community or broader cultural context, so that people in the future will understand the many layers of value to your stories.

As we discussed early on in this workbook, your food memories are part of a larger human story. Our life stories, which include our food stories, tend to parallel larger societal trends. As representatives of larger communities our stories help document community movements and a larger social history.

For example, during our childhoods, we went out to eat less. We sat at a family table more. Our individual experiences reflected the times on these matters, but other things differed because we grew up in different places and have different ethnic backgrounds. Bagels and matzo balls were normal for Melissa in her communities. Rice Krispy treats and tuna with peas on toast were normal for Sue.

Consider sharing your food stories with your local historical society or library to help document your communities and your times. Cultural heritage organizations such as these have the interest and facilities to keep and preserve your memories for a bigger community. After all, *we* make today's culture, to the historians of the future. Work together to develop ways to share and preserve your stories for posterity. Identify the stories and expertise in your community that should be passed down. Leave behind evidence that you were here, of your role in a larger world and the influence of your community culture.

> "Food is our common ground, a universal experience."
>
> - **James Beard (American Chef and food writer)**

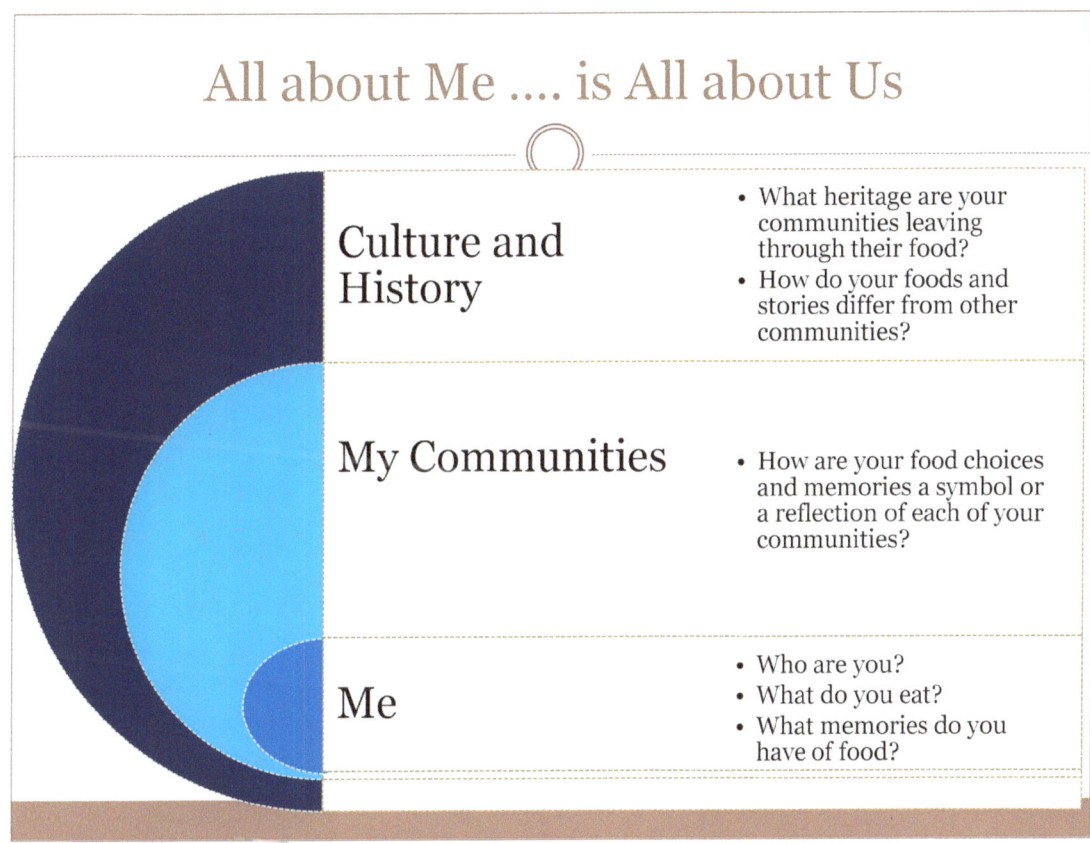

Figure 12 In this diagram, we show that our memories, even though they are personal, live in a broader context.

Entries from our food memories contest beginning on page 37 demonstrate what food can say about you, your communities and your culture. Each writer saw our sample stories (pages 11-14) and used our questions (found on page 8) as a launching point to answer **"Why do we eat the things we eat and how do our meals reflect our life in context?"** Their memories are fascinating, beautiful and enlightening. We hope that they provide a little more inspiration for you to record your own.

Sample 5: Sue's Family Recipe Boxes, in Context

The Recipe Boxes

In Sue's home, she keeps a recipe binder with her household's favorite recipes. These come from those with whom she lives, from her mother, from friends, and from online recipes she tries.

Also kept in the same area are two recipe boxes to which no new cards are ever added. For the most part, these recipes stay in their original homes, in these two recipe boxes, in honor of the two women who created them. The only recipes moved are the "holiday" recipes; because they are easier for Sue to locate in her regular big binder. For preservation purposes, the cards can be copied and placed in the binder with originals kept in the recipe boxes. (This is a useful example of how we all organize differently and need to pay attention to how we think about organization to easily find things.)

The pictured green metal recipe box is from Sue's grandmother. Sue's childhood memories are of wonderful meals and special foods, when Baba and Sue visited. Later in life, her grandmother preferred to eat out rather than cook in. So having Baba's recipe box from her young married days is a special treat. Also fascinating is simply reading these recipes, because most foods we no longer make, but they describe what Baba's cooking included: Tuna fish fry, Welsh rarebit, English tea cakes.

The pink plastic recipe box is of "Meme's" recipes. Meme is actually Sue's housemate's mother, who passed away in 2008. Meme, though, treated Sue like her own daughter. Meme was French and her husband Portuguese, so the recipe box has recipes from both traditions. And, those were the days when the French married only the French, and the Portuguese only married the Portuguese, in their city. It's also very special to see her handwriting, because it's as if she is still here.

Figure 13 Sue's recipe boxes

Sue's recipe boxes are a perfect collection. They tell us a lot about the people who created them. Archivists will do as Sue as done and retain the collection intact, not mixing recipes or papers passed down from different people. Keeping them separate allows us to get a glimpse into a particular person's life. We can imagine Sue's Baba and Meme working in the kitchen with their own recipe boxes in front of them.

The recipes are fun to read even if you aren't going to make them. Such a collection becomes more interesting and informative if one writes and keeps a short biography about the original cook at the front of the box. Include the birth and death date of the person and a photo of the person. Pass the collection down in your bequests later in life.

One thing to keep in mind: recipe cards are often made of poor quality paper.[7] To ensure that the recipes and the sense of the original owner of the recipes are maintained, make copies of the cards. Take a photograph of an original box so you always remember how it looks as an "artifact" and store the original using archival supplies.[6] Scan or photocopy each recipe card so, if the original does start to deteriorate, the information stays intact and the way it looks can be remembered forever. There are many ways that you can keep these copies. Print a book of them using an online company such as Shutterfly or Createspace, make a CD of scans, or just keep a duplicate paper file of the recipes.[7]

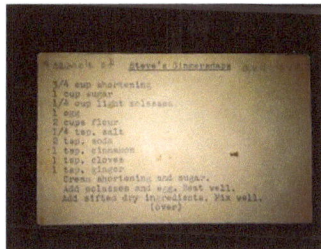

Figure 14 Sue's recipe card shows the yellowing that is common on cards that are often used for recipes. The card will become brittle over time and should be copied for safekeeping.

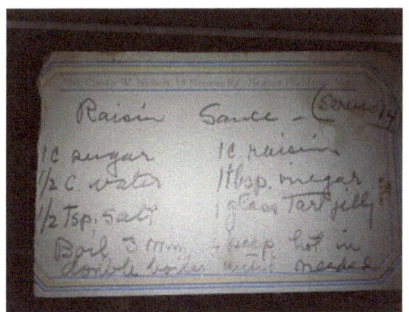

Figure 15 A recipe card from Sue's collection even reveals her great grandmother's handwriting

---

[7] For more on maintaining and safely preserving family papers see Melissa Mannon's book *The Unofficial Family Archivist: A Guide to Creating and Maintaining Family Papers, Photographs, and Memorabilia*. NH: ArchivesInfo, 2011.
[6] See footnote on page 26 for a list of reputable archival supply companies.
[7] There are many online companies that allow you to duplicate, protect, and bind your family information in clever ways. Shutterfly and Createspace are two of Melissa's favorites. See: http://www.shutterfly.com and http://www.createspace.com

Worksheet: Cultural Context

How can your food memories be put into a cultural context? Are your food memories rooted to your ethnicity or your geographic locale?

_____

_____

_____

What aspects of your food stories reflect the times in which you have lived?

_____

_____

_____

What other information about a particular food memory would you be interested to learn? Who in your community could you reach out to fill gaps in your memories -- in your family or beyond?

_____

_____

_____

What additional information about your food memories would others want to know? What would people who want to learn about your communities need to hear to understand how food has influenced you and your loved ones?

_____

_____

_____

Maple Syrup   by Erica Holthausen

New England winters can be interminable. By the time February rolls around, the skies are gray and the snow is brown. March shows signs of warmer weather as thin sheets of ice stretch across the frozen mud. I understand why some people don't like this time of year. But when I was growing up, the weeks between Presidents' Day and St. Patrick's Day were a sweet, golden amber dream known as maple syrup season.

By age seven, I was an integral part of the sugaring operations at Maple Grove Farm in North Guilford, Connecticut. Maple sugaring was a family affair, and each one of us had a role to play. I was the tour guide, and I took my job very seriously. I would show visitors the sap buckets and collection tanks, let them taste the clear, sugar-water-flavored sap and explain the entire sugaring off process. Everything I knew I had learned from my grandfather, whom I adored. He taught me that it was the Native Americans who shared the secrets of maple syrup production with our ancestors, even though there were plenty of sugar maples in Europe. He taught me that the sap runs when cold nights alternate with warm days – and that the sap stops running when the leaves start developing. Finally, he taught me the show stopping statistic that was guaranteed to get a low whistle: it takes 40 gallons of sap to make just one gallon of syrup.

While I loved being a tour guide, the best time of day was after the visitors left. My cousins, nine and eleven, and I would go with my grandfather to collect the sap. The two boys would dump buckets of sap into the collection tank on the trailer. I sat with my grandfather, occasionally steering the big green John Deere tractor through the fields. As the sun set, we would finish collecting the sap and head back to the sugar house. Sometimes we'd have pancakes for dinner, with a little bit of hot maple syrup drawn right from the evaporator. Other times we'd have chili or stew – which meant that dessert would be a maple syrup taffy made by pouring maple syrup onto fresh snow and letting it chill enough to become a sweet, flexible treat.

My grandfather died in 1984, a few months shy of my tenth birthday. As good Yankees, we didn't talk about everything we had lost. Instead, we tapped trees, hung buckets, strung up tubing and stacked the wood that would fuel the evaporator. These simple acts gave us a sense of purpose and brought us together at a time when the strain of caring for my grandmother, who had severe Alzheimer's, threatened to tear the family apart completely. In that small sugar house, over stacks of pancakes smothered in hot syrup, we shared our stories – breaking with one tradition while upholding another.

See Erica's website at: http://www.honestmarketingrevolution.com

Boxed Treasures   by Amber B.

I learned to love cooking from my Grandmother. In my eyes, her cooking was effortless, resulting in a chorus of "mmmmm's" at the table. Every favorite meal, flavor, treat, canned item, or condiment recipe was in my Grandmothers keep. I thought her recipes were mainly clippings from newspapers or magazines. They were the only ones I ever saw with her. I had no idea she was carrying on a family tradition herself. She was preserving her family memories and going back in time with every bite of a recipe made from her childhood.

It always made me feel so loved and welcomed when I would visit and she had one of my favorite meals made. One favorite casserole was simply titled 'Beef n Noodle Bake'. At Christmas you had to check the refrigerator in the garage; Grandmother kept the good stuff there. There were Peanut Butter Balls dipped in chocolate, kept in a wax paper lined coffee can, alongside at least five other cans of different cookies. Grandmother was also gifted at canning -- Bread n Butter pickles, Garlic Dill pickles, Sweet Relish, Jams, Jellies, and more were canned fresh from her garden, which she cared for with so much pride.

Grandmother passed away in 1995 when I was twenty-four. She was my first relative to pass. At the house after her funeral Grandfather came to me with a green felt box. It was my Grandmothers' wedding ring set. Family legend says that the band had been passed down through three generations. I was thankful and overwhelmed, but it wasn't what I thought I really wanted as a memory. I walked the halls of Grandmother's house. I stared at pictures on walls and softly touched every owl item she collected. I admired her delicate cross-stitch, giggled at her piles of cheesy romance novels, and thumbed through all her sewing patterns.

I mustered the courage to ask my Grandfather for one more thing from my Grandmother -- her recipe boxes. One box was metal, painted white, with orange and yellow flowers scattered over it. The hinge was rusting and crumbs dusted the bottom. The other is a sturdy green, slightly grimy plastic box. I eventually let go of the metal box since it was falling apart. While I was transferring those recipe cards, I noticed they weren't all newspaper or magazine clippings. Over eighty-percent were handwritten. What was more endearing to me was that Grandmother wrote the name of the person from whom she received each recipe. Those names took on greater importance to me in my genealogy research. There were recipes from her mom, aunts, and sister in laws. Learning that earned those recipes a place in my will, digital copies on my hard drive and stories I share with my family.

My oldest son enjoys working with me in the kitchen and I've shared with him my precious box. We have since added his favorite recipe. Soon we will add his younger brothers. I look forward to hearing one day, 'Mom, I will be home this weekend, I can't wait to have some home cooking.'

Food Memories   by Heather Jaremko

My food memories are of lemonade slurpies which my mother would prepare when my sister and I got home from school on a hot day. It would also be served to guests. This drink used a whole can of lemonade. We added some water and ice cubes and blended until all of the ice was broken down. It was what we would call a slurpie today.

My food memories also include my mother-in-law's family three layer birthday chocolate cake. This cake is an easy family staple and can survive through anything. I remember one time when I made this recipe and forgot to separate the egg whites to beat up separately and add to the batter after everything else was combined. As it turned out, my husband and I didn't really see any difference. The cake baked just as well as if the egg whites had been folded in.

I made this chocolate cake one summer and we put it in the back of our car on the floor, so that it would not get too much direct sunlight. We decided to drive the south route to White Rock, B.C. to visit my mother and father who were living out there at this particular time. We had been driving over 11 hours and when we got to my parent's home, and took the top off the cake keeper, the cake was just fine. This trip was made in July and the weather was really hot. We had some of the cake the following day, as it was after 11 p.m. when we arrived to see my mother and father. We were visiting with my parents for a while and managed to eat all the cake before coming back to Calgary.

Other food memories were of my husband making a tuna cashew casserole and bringing it down to our apartment. He had a home near Confederation Park and he would go back to the house during the day to do work and then come to the apartment. My husband was renting rooms in his home at the time we got married. We moved into the house after our honeymoon in July. We were married in March. On this particular occasion, he parked in the parking lot at the apartment complex and was taking the casserole out of the car, when it fell on the ground and even the dish which he had the casserole in broke. He spent quite some time picking everything up and putting it into the dumpster. We ended up doing something different for dinner that night.

Grandma Gailey Made Do   by Judith Richards Shubert

As kids we used to always go to "Seven Mile Park" for picnics. I remember when I was just a little girl the entire family would pack up in the car and drive the few miles south of town for a picnic and an Easter egg hunt. It was a beautiful place – full of rocks to climb and places to hide. There was a view to die for. I remember when I came back home after being married and living away in other states I was disappointed that the view that we had enjoyed was marred by taller trees and bushes, obscuring the wonderful Texas rolling hills that are so beautiful. I thought the least the Texas Department of Highways could do was to preserve that view! Guess I was wrong. You still can't see for miles like you could when I was a child.

Grandma used to pack up boxes with fried chicken, deviled eggs, potato salad, cakes and cupcakes. I don't remember what the picnic basket looked like, but I imagine it was a cardboard box, not a fancy wicker basket.

She made wonderful potato salad and I make it the same way – with pickle relish, celery, onions, pimento, boiled eggs, mayonnaise and mustard mixed into potatoes that have been creamed with milk and butter. Yum!

I hope I expressed to Grandma my gratitude for the food she always prepared for us as kids. She always had something good to eat when we came home from school and on the weekends. She didn't have a lot of money – but neither did a lot of people back in the early 50s. I remember many times when she would send me up to the corner store to buy one onion, or a can of tomatoes so she could make her wonderful vegetable soup. She didn't use meat. The soup was a make-do meal that she served with fantastic cornbread. (I still can't make that cornbread like she did.)

Anyway, I was remembering Grandma this morning and how she "made-do" and how we as Americans are learning a little more about that in this particular time in history.

Show your gratitude. Tell your parents and grandparents thank you! I wish I had done that more often.

See more writing by Judith at: http://genealogytraces.blogspot.com and http://foodgratitude.blogspot.com

Little Pizzas   by Carrie Mcintyre

Little pizzas are made with English muffins, pizza sauce, grated cheese, pepperoni, and whatever other toppings you like. We would add sliced black olives and Italian sausage. It was one of the first foods I learned to cook on my own as a child.

I remember being taught how to make these by my 2nd grade teacher, Mrs Hammond. She was a big busty woman with gray hair, and wore dresses. She looked a little like Aunt Bee from the Andy Griffith show. At the end of the week she would lead our class in square dances. But this was California in the early 1970s, so learning how to make little pizzas was a concession to modern times!

Once we learned how to make them – basically, you just layer the muffin and stick it in the oven until the cheese melts – we 7 year olds took our new found knowledge home and badgered our mothers to let us cook them. So it is my mother who I really associate with this food. She used to make homemade pizza, taking us to a local Italian deli in our Willys jeep to get fresh dough, mozzarella cheese, and fresh, spicy, Italian sausage and pepperoni. I remember walking down the aisles of the deli looking at all the strange products and the doughy smell of the shop. The Willys was an old green jeep. It was the precursor to today's SUV wagons. We had to tug on a rope to get the windshield wipers to work when it rained. It had no seatbelts or other modern safety devices. I have many fond memories of laying down either on the back seat or in the very back of the jeep behind the seats and looking up out the windows while we drove home from various visits, watching the moving night sky.

My mom's homemade pizza was the best. She made her own sauce. We never ate the canned stuff. Even for spaghetti, the sauce was also made from scratch. So the little pizzas were a way for Mom to spend time with us in the kitchen and involve us in the cooking. It also allowed her to do less work than she would when she made the normal pizzas, especially because she skipped the oven and would let us pop the pizza muffins into the microwave. It was a quick and easy kid friendly meal.

I've never written about this memory before; there might be a recipe card in my mother's kitchen but I doubt it. It was so long ago.

Culturally I think this shows a glimpse of the diverse world we lived in. We aren't Italian, though we cooked Italian foods and shopped in Italian shops. Nor were we Okies or from the world Andy Griffith depicted – although my parents would have been the children of that world and generation. We were the product of California, which was a conglomeration of everyone. Culturally my memory is more of a time and era overlap than any ethnicity. And that history, that sense of time, has definitely shaped who I am today -- the American mutt.

Christmas Pudding   by Sally Kemball-Cook

The process would begin in June. My Grandmother always picked the morning of what promised to be a sweltering day to make that year's Christmas Pudding in her small, Darien, Connecticut kitchen. If I were lucky, my parents would let me visit so I could watch the process unfold. Christmas Pudding is a traditional British pudding that is served…you guessed it…on Christmas day after the "required meal" of Roast Beef and Yorkshire Pudding. It was a way for my Grandmother, a southern woman through and through, to honor my Grandfather's British heritage.

The ingredient list is long, daunting and involves ingredients such as bread crumbs, beef suet, ale, carrots, raisins, walnuts, cherries, plums and rum. Let's not forget the rum! The rum is what made the entire process fascinating for me. That's because once Grandmother assembled and cooked the pudding for 10 hours on that hot June day, she would let it cool and add A LOT of rum. The pudding would take a Mount Gay Rum (only Mount Gay mind you as it was Grandmother's favorite) bath for six…yes six…months until it was debuted on December 25.

On Christmas Day it was always my job to make the traditional Hard Sauce accompaniment. Hard Sauce is best described as sweet, firm vanilla icing and it's essential if you're a child who has to choke down a serving of Christmas Pudding every year. About 3 hours before the evening meal my Grandmother would bring out the pudding. She would carefully remove it from its rum bath and place it on the stove to steam until we were ready to serve. Once we finished dinner it was my job to place the pudding on a large serving platter and gently warm more rum to pour over the top. Now I was only supposed to use a ½ cup of rum but I would always sneak a little extra. Why? That's because the next step in the process is what I waited all year to see and the more rum I added the longer it would take. After I added the extra rum my father would turn off the lights and I would set a match to the Christmas Pudding. Spectacular blue flames would erupt and I would carefully walk the pudding to the dining room and pass the platter to my Grandmother. She would gently swirl the rum on the platter in an attempt to keep the pudding in flames as long as possible. After several minutes the blue flames would die out and we would all cheer the spectacular pudding and effort that had gone into making it. My Grandmother would then place the platter in front of my Grandfather to serve.

Many years after the death of my Grandparents the tradition lives on in my family. Every June several family members begin the arduous process of creating that year's Christmas Pudding. Oftentimes we are not able to celebrate the holiday together but the phone always rings off the hook on Christmas night to discuss each pudding and how it turned out. I am not particularly fond of the dish, but I anticipate that first bite each year because it takes me back to my childhood and makes me feel that my Grandparents are right there beside me.

See Sally's food blog at at: http://www.theriskykitchen.com

French Meat Pies   by Donna Enos Burke

Back to the days of my great, great grandmother at least, our family has enjoyed the tradition of the making of French meat pies for a traditional New Year's Day party. The tradition originated with our family in Melansonville, Nova Scotia. These days, I make the family meat pies with my two oldest nephews. They have no idea how unique they are, in this tradition.

Tradition says that the matriarchs make the meat pies, and the children do not assist. The females wait their turn which is when the current matriarchs can no longer handle the responsibility. So my grandmother (Memere) made the meat pies with her sister, Aunt Leonie, until the ends of their lives. My mom, Yvette took over, with her sister, Dot. I could watch, with my younger brother, but we never helped because that was not our role. Making the meat pies indicated who the matriarchs were, and they were strong women, my family. Back then, the women made 30-35 meat pies. It's a lot, yes, but even more of a feat when you know that the pies were made in a kitchenette. That room measures about 4 ½ feet square.

When the meat pies are ready for storage, we put them on the front porch. And each year, another part of our meat pies tradition is to pray for cold weather – not cold enough to freeze the pies, but cold enough to keep the meat fresh! These days, the porch is glassed in, but it was open air back in the day.

My dad was the first male to help make pies. My mother was the last surviving female of her generation, so as she aged and had health issues he got involved, although she supervised and did what she could. As gentle and loving as he was in taking care of my mom, he also used those skills as he took on a role in meat pie cooking. He is Portuguese, and back then, the marriage of a French woman and Portuguese man was frowned upon, and nearly disallowed by the church and their families. So this was, indeed, a special honor he was given, on many levels.

I am the first to involve children. My two eldest, twin nephews helped make the meat pies beginning at the age of seven. We have great fun as we discuss life at their age and love the time we spend, just us. Last year, it was a discussion of how we'd structure our French meat pie making business. Who the CEO, CFO and chief baker would be. My housemate has helped for as long as I have made the meat pies. And my cousin has also helped. So we've mixed it up a bit, but we continue the tradition every year.

We share the pie outside family. My dad's social group meets at the local McDonald's almost daily. They go out dancing and take field trips together. So he has a new tradition based on meat pies. He has a party for his group and it's in February near the date of my mother's passing. He serves meat pies; we make extra for just this purpose. I love that we honor her in this way.

Special ingredients: My meme's friend first did this. She had run out of milk to brush on the crusts so that when you pinch the bottom and top crusts together, they stay together. She licked her two fingers and pinched! So, just to be funny, each year, my meme, my mother and now I lick our fingers for one pie crust, honoring a tradition!

Each year, dad finds the best price for ground pork. I pull out the recipe in my mother's handwriting. We discuss many times how we're going to find the time to travel to dad's so we can boil the meat in time but not too early (an hours-long process), and how many pies we'll be making this year.

I took on the tradition at a mere 50 years old, so I had still waited a long time for the privilege! And now, each year, we have the pleasure of "my boys" joining us to carry on our traditions, just in quite a different way from the family ever imagined, back in Melansonville, Nova Scotia.

Your reminiscences and recordings of them can be a collaborative effort. Sometimes, they transform into more extensive projects. Here's Donna's story about the writing of "French Meat Pies":

> *Sue [West] interviewed my dad and me before the Christmas holidays. I couldn't wait to tell my nephews what I'd learned, simply because it was the two us sharing our own memories of the same tradition.*
>
> *In my family, I was raised in a household with my parents, brother and my grandparents. Relatives stopped by frequently; our home was open to all. Because of this, you'd expect that I know all my family stories. And I do know a lot of stories, but it's the perspectives of other people involved in the same tradition which makes this so rich an experience.*
>
> *My mom died almost four years ago now. Fairly often, "my boys" (the two older nephews who knew her) will ask questions about their Meme, their grandmother. They know we used to make the meat pies together. The house they live in was originally built for my mom and dad, but she passed away before the house was finished.*
>
> *This meat pies story and what I learned from this story interview have inspired me to make a Meme History Book for my boys. The binder will have photos, family recipes, something about her faith and strength, maybe something about the "house that Meme built," favorite stories, gestures and sayings she had, particularly with "my boys."*
>
> *So I'd encourage everyone to tell your stories and listen to what others in your family say about the same stories.*

What's Next? Share Your Memories.

Consider how you can continue to create, organize, and record more food memories. Make them an important part of your community. Here are some ideas for what to do next:

- Simple but powerful gifts of heritage. Share your stories with family. Type up your stories on pretty paper and give the stories as a gift. Add photos of the food or related items, too!

- Choose a fellow foodie. Who in your family shows interest in family history or in cooking? Choose that one person and begin telling your stories, cooking family recipes together, and discovering new ways to record your memories *together.*

- Make your own family cookbook. Pull together your favorite recipes and favorite stories. Invite other family members to write their stories or interview them to help elicit memories. Create a Print on Demand book to share with family. Lulu.com and Createspace.com are great POD companies for creating your own books. Shutterfly and Snapfish are companies focused on photo products.

- Have a party with friends. Whether you host a kitchen products party or simply gather friends together, make a theme of recording favorite food memories. You can write them, scrapbook them or even record or videotape the section of the party when you each tell your story.

- Support your local historical society, library, small business or charity by arranging a community event to explore and sample favorite recipes and family food stories.

- Start a recipe mailing. Make a list of ten people to whom you can send a recipe and ask them to mail a recipe to you plus ten other people, too.

- Do some research at your local historical society. See what food related stories might be hidden in their collections.

- Organize your recipe collection. Highlight the recipes you use most often. Note the ones that your family most enjoys or that you make on special occasions. Make notes directly on the recipes not only about your experience making the recipe, but who you made it for and when. This becomes a family journal!

- At each holiday, encourage people to tell and pass on stories to the group that's gathered. Take on the role of recorder of food memories to get everyone involved and excited about the project. You may even find some volunteers!

- Reevaluate your kitchen as a place to make family food memories. How can you make use of the space to promote traditions. Make sure you have baking supplies on hand for a rainy day that you might spend in the kitchen baking with family. Buy special cookie cutters for holidays and keep them stored neatly so they are easily accessible.

- Create a "Thanksgiving Food Tree" in early November. Draw a tree trunk on a large piece of paper and draw (or trace) leaf shapes onto colorful papers. Cut out the leaves and leave them in a basket near your tree trunk with some nearby tape. Encourage family members to write at least one food memory for which they are thankful and tape it to the tree. Encourage visitors to fill out leaves. Call long-distance relatives and tell them about the tree. Ask them about their food memories and write a leaf for them OR mail out leaves to family members and ask them to mail them back with a written memory on them.

What other activities would allow you to share your food memories? Make a list of creative projects you would like to start to explore these memories:

_____

_____

_____

_____

_____

_____

Would You Like to Share What You Have Explored Here?

Sue West and Melissa Mannon encourage you to share your stories and your methods for documenting them. Through their "Life in Context" Facebook page, workshop participants can continue to explore the ideas we've discussed here.

- Are you interested in continuing your "Life in Context" work with a family member? Purchase more workshop books from Sue or Melissa.

- Would you like to arrange to have "A Life in Context: Telling Your Story" workshop at your institution or in your town?

- Would you like to stay abreast of the latest news about organizing your life and/or preserving history and building community memories?

- Would you like to learn more about services and events offered by Space4U and ArchivesInfo online and in your community?

Contact: info@lifeincontext.org

Want to stay connected? Sign up for our newsletters. Join our Facebook pages. Visit our blogs. Follow us on Twitter or on LinkedIn!

Sue West –
- Sue@OrganizeNH.com
- www.organizenh.com
- www.OrganizeForAFreshStart.com
- www.facebook.com/SueWestOrganizingCoach
- @Space4U on Twitter
- LinkedIn: http://www.linkedin.com/in/suewestspace4u

Melissa Mannon -
- Melissa@archivesinfo.com
- www.archivesinfo.com
- archivesinfo.blogspot.com
- www.facebook.com/archivesinfo
- @archivesinfo on Twitter
- LinkedIn: http://www.linkedin.com/in/melissamannon

"Melissa is a true professional, with deep knowledge of both her field and its applications to so many different situations." – Sarah Brophy, Museum Consultant, BMuse

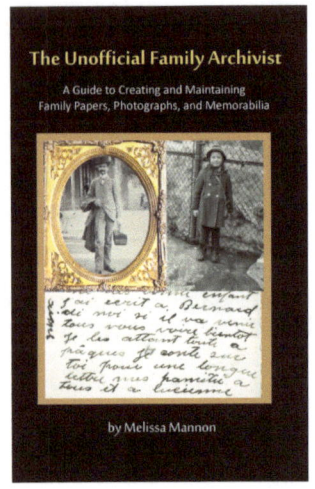

The Unofficial Family Archivist

Cultural Heritage Collaborators

*Melissa Mannon, Author
MSLS, Archivist and
Cultural Heritage Consultant*

Highlight your life story. Explore your communities.

Treasure your documentation.
It is the key to knowledge, memory and identity.

"In short order Melissa argues a convincing case for the centrality of archival records for the public good…" - Ryan Lewis, Program Officer - Outreach & Programs, Illinois Humanities Council. review of *Cultural Heritage Collaborators*.

Learn more or purchase the books

http://www.archivesinfo.com/unofficialarch.php

http://www.archivesinfo.com/culturalcollab.php

Melissa@ArchivesInfo.com
603-661-7611

Blog: archivesinfo.blogspot.com
Web Site: ArchivesInfo.com
On Twitter and Google+ as ArchivesInfo

Sue West, Author
Certified Organizer Coach®
Certified Professional Organizer®

Big life changes?
Not sure what's next?
Regroup. Remember. Reorganize.
Gain some control.
Come out of the fog.

> *"West has written on a topic dear to my heart—*
> *getting organized to cope with and*
> *embrace change and transition.*
>
> *A great roadmap."*
>
> *Endorsed by Judith Kolberg, Publisher, Book Coach, International Speaker*

Preview or Purchase the Book

www.OrganizeForAFreshStart.com

Sue@OrganizeNH.com
603.554.1948 (Office)
603.765.9267 (Cell)

Blog: www.OrganizeForAFreshStart.com
Organizing & Coaching Site: www.OrganizeNH.com

www.ingramcontent.com/pod-product-compliance
Lightning Source LLC
Chambersburg PA
CBHW060758090426
42736CB00002B/73